HAL•LEONARD

pro**Vocal**®
BETTER THAN KARAOKE!

MOVIE SONGS

ISBN-13: 978-1-4234-3194-7
ISBN-10: 1-4234-3194-4

HAL•LEONARD®
CORPORATION

7777 W. BLUEMOUND RD. P.O. BOX 13819 MILWAUKEE, WI 53213

Visit Hal Leonard Online at
www.halleonard.com

MOVIE SONGS

CONTENTS

Could I Have This Dance

from URBAN COWBOY

Words and Music by Wayland Holyfield and Bob House

Chorus

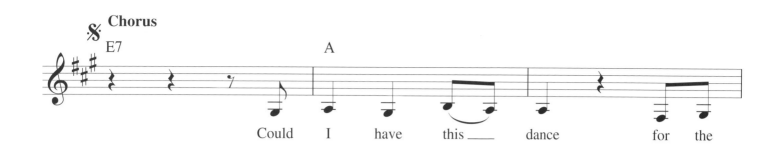

Could I have this ____ dance for the

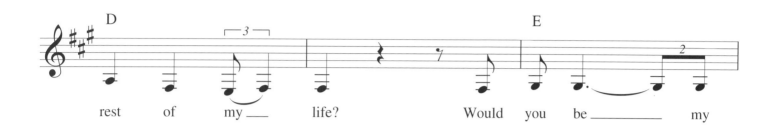

rest of my ___ life? Would you be _____ my

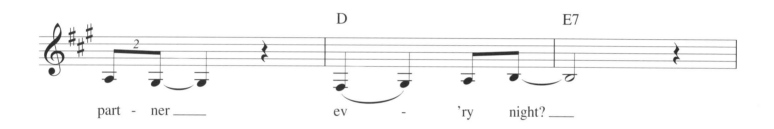

part - ner _____ ev - 'ry night? ____

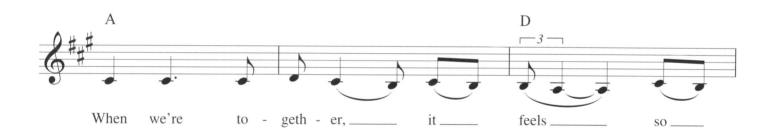

When we're to - geth - er, _____ it ____ feels _____ so ___

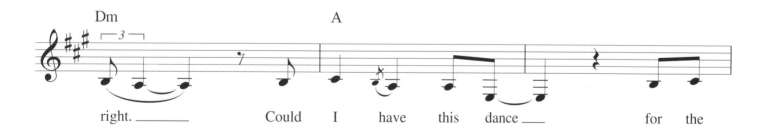

right. _____ Could I have this dance ___ for the

To Coda ⊕

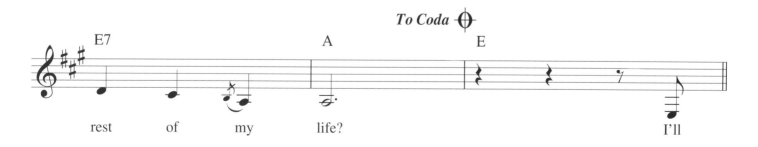

rest of my life? I'll

5

Verse

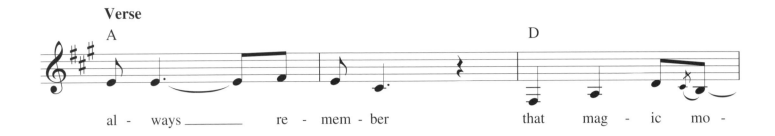

al - ways _____ re - mem - ber   that   mag - ic   mo -

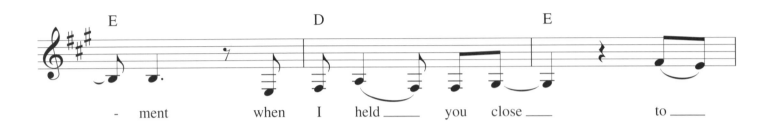

- ment   when   I   held _____ you   close _____ to _____

me.   As   we   moved _____ to -

geth - er   I   knew _____ for - ev - er, _____

D.S. al Coda

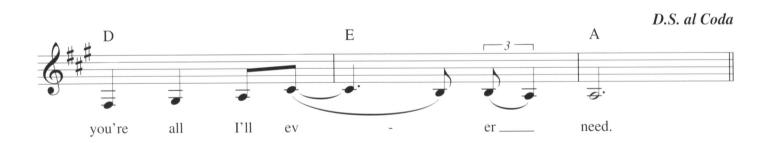

you're   all   I'll   ev   -   er _____ need.

Coda   **Chorus**

Could   I   have   this _____

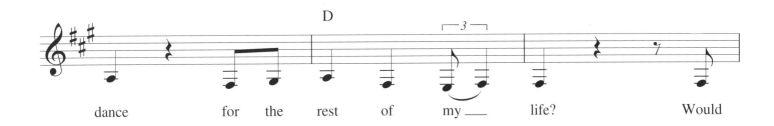

dance   for   the   rest   of   my ___   life?   Would

you   be _____   my   part - ner _____   ev -   'ry   night? _

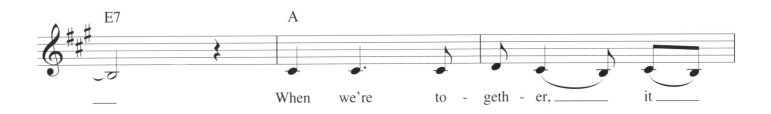

___   When   we're   to - geth - er, _____   it _____

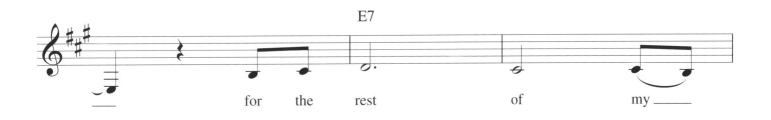

feels _____   so ____   right. _____   Could   I   have   this   dance _

___   for   the   rest   of   my _____

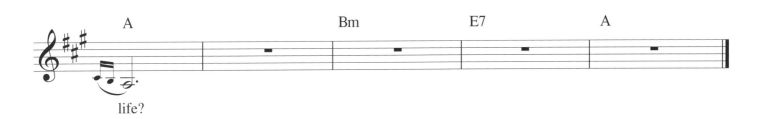

life?

Hopelessly Devoted to You

from GREASE

Words and Music by John Farrar

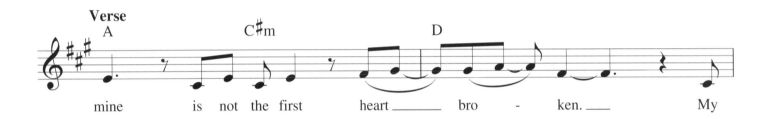

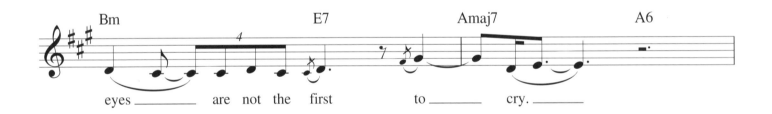

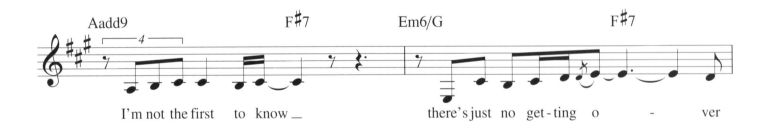

Verse

lone, I'm just a fool _ who's _ will - ing to

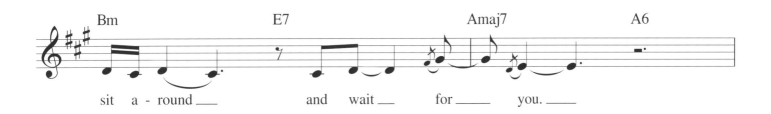

sit a - round ___ and wait __ for ____ you. ___

but ba - by, can't you see there's noth - ing else for me ____ to

do? _____ I'm hope - less - ly de - vot - ed _____

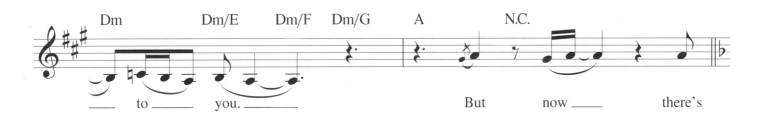

___ to ____ you. _____ But now ___ there's

Bridge

no - where to hide since you pushed my love a - side. _ I'm _

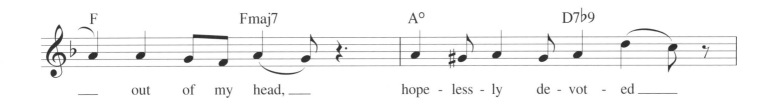

___ out of my head, ___ hope - less - ly de - vot - ed _____

9

to __ you, _____ hope - less - ly de - vot - ed _____

to you, _____ hoo, _____ hoo, _____ hoo,

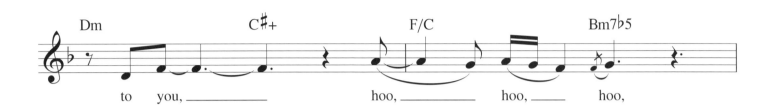

hope - less - ly de - vot - ed _____ to you. _____

Verse

_____ 3. My head is say - in', "fool, _____

_____ for - get him." _____ My heart is say - in', "Don't let him __

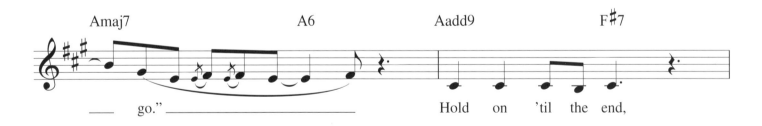

_____ go." _____ Hold on 'til the end,

that's what I in - tend _____ to do. _____ I'm

hope - less - ly de - vot - ed _____ to _____ you. _____

Bridge

But now there's no - where to hide since you

pushed my love a - side. __ I'm __ out of my head, __

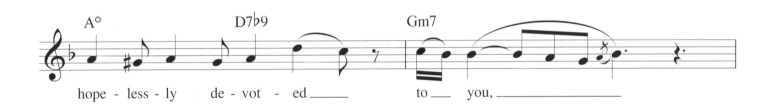

hope - less - ly de - vot - ed _____ to __ you, _____

hope - less - ly de - vot - ed _____ to you, _____ hoo, __

hoo, hoo, _____ hoo. Hope - less - ly de - vot - ed _____

to you, _____ ooh.

I Will Always Love You

from THE BODYGUARD
Words and Music by Dolly Parton

you.   I   will al - ways love

you.   You,   my dar -

- ling, you.   Mm.   2. Bit - ter -

Verse

- sweet   mem - o - ries,   that is

all I'm tak - ing with   me.   So good -

- bye,   please   don't   cry. We   both

  know I'm   not what you,   you need.   And I

13

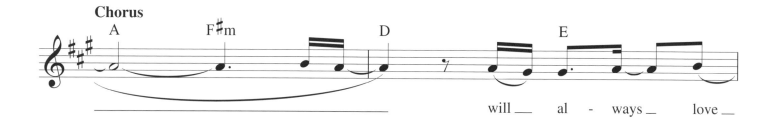

Chorus

will _ al - ways _ love _

_ you. _ I _____ will _ al - ways _ love _

Bridge

_ you. _____

Verse

3. I _____ hope _____ life ___ treats _ you _

_ kind, _____ and I hope ___ you have all _ you _ dreamed _

D   E   A   E/A

__ of. _____ And I wish __ you joy ____ and __ hap - pi -

A   C#m7   F#m   C#m/E

ness. _____ But a - bove all __ this   I ____ wish you ____ love. __

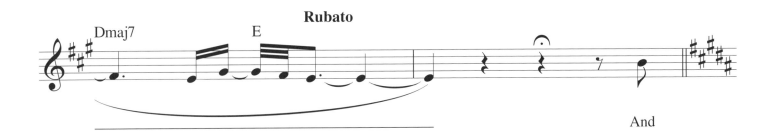

Dmaj7   E   **Rubato**

_____ And

Chorus

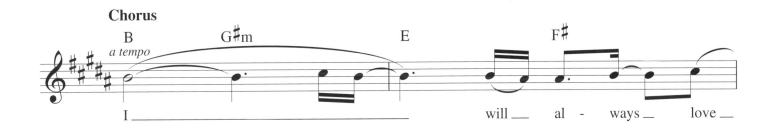

B   *a tempo*   G#m   E   F#

I _____ will __ al - ways __ love __

B   G#m   C#m   F#

__ you. _____ I __ will al - ways __ love ____

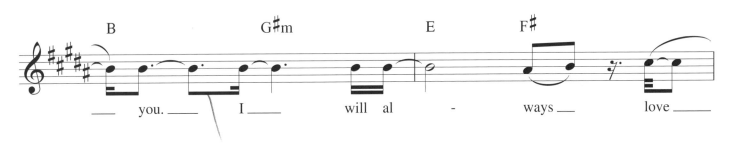

B   G#m   E   F#

__ you. __ I ___ will al - ways __ love __

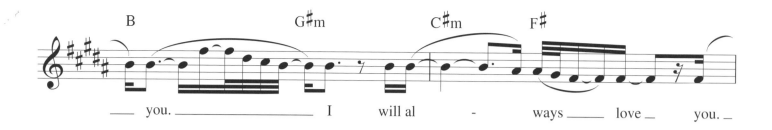

B   G#m   C#m   F#

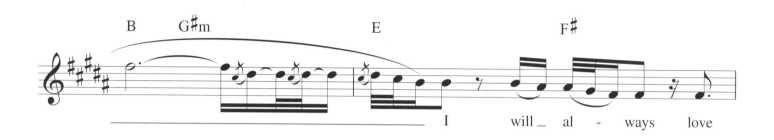

___ you. ___ I will al - ways ___ love ___ you. ___

B   G#m   E   F#

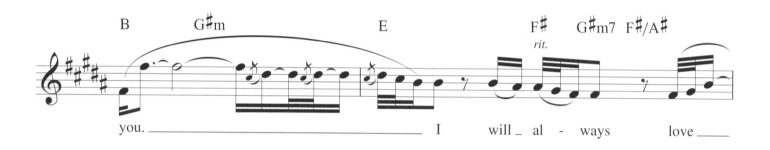

_____ I will ___ al - ways love

B   G#m   E   F#   G#m7   F#/A#

rit.

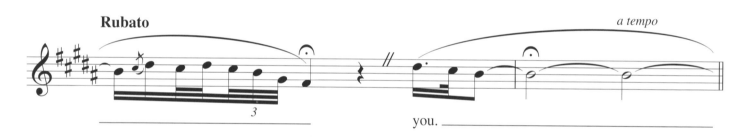

you. ___ I will ___ al - ways love ___

Rubato   *a tempo*

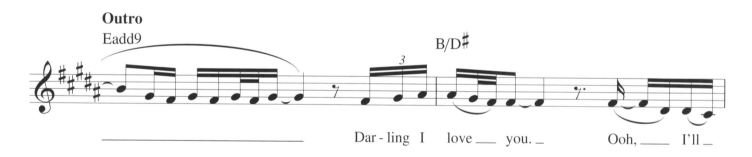

3   you. ___

Outro

Eadd9   *3*   B/D#

_____ Dar - ling I love ___ you. ___ Ooh, ___ I'll ___

Rubato

F#sus4   F#   Badd9

6

al - ways, I'll ___ al - ways ___ love ___ you. _____

I Will Remember You

Theme from THE BROTHERS McMULLEN

Words and Music by Sarah McLachlan, Seamus Egan and Dave Merenda

Intro-Chorus
Moderately slow

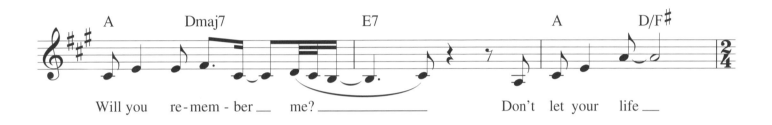

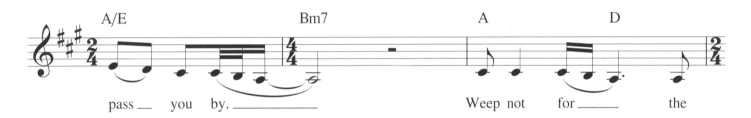

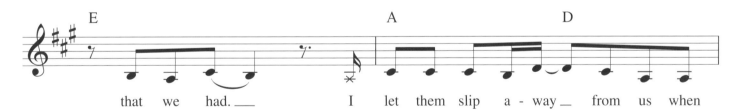

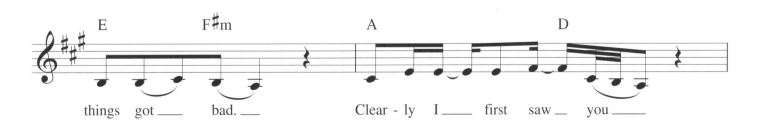

smil - in' in ___ the sun.   I wan - na feel ___ your warmth up - on ___ me.   I

Chorus

wan - na be   the one.   I _____ will re - mem - ber ___ you. ___

Will you re - mem - ber ___ me? _____ Don't

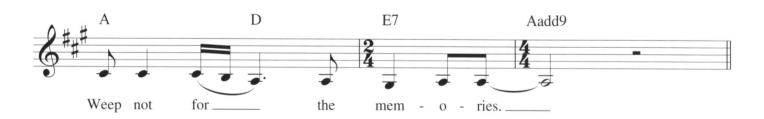

let your life ___   pass ___ you by. _____

Weep not   for _____ the mem - o - ries. _____

Verse

2. I'm ___ so ___ tired ___   that I can't sleep.

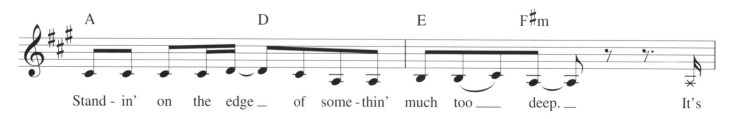

Stand - in' on the edge ___ of some - thin' much too ___ deep. ___   It's

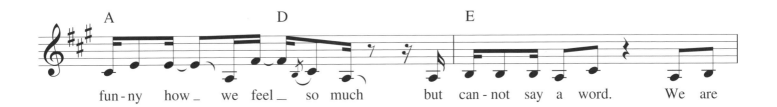

fun - ny how _ we feel _ so much but can - not say a word. We are

scream - ing in - side, _ oh, _____ we can't be heard. I _

Chorus

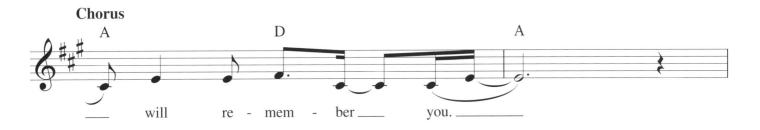

_ will re - mem - ber _ you. _____

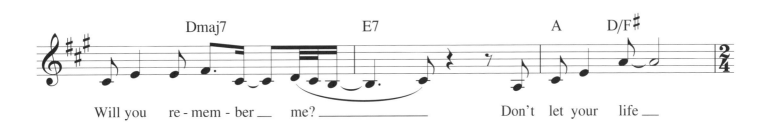

Will you re - mem - ber _ me? _____ Don't let your life _

pass _ you by. _____ Weep not for _____ the

Interlude

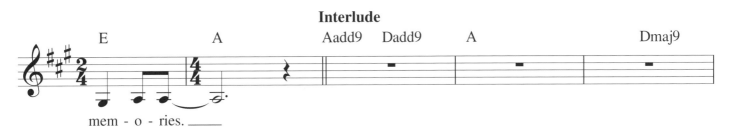

mem - o - ries. _____

Verse

3. So a - fraid _ to love _ you, more a - fraid _ to lose. _

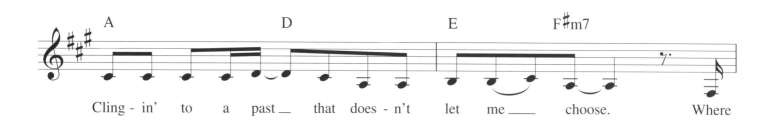

Cling - in' to a past _ that does - n't let me ___ choose. Where

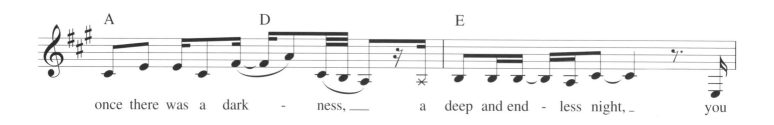

once there was a dark - ness, ___ a deep and end - less night, _ you

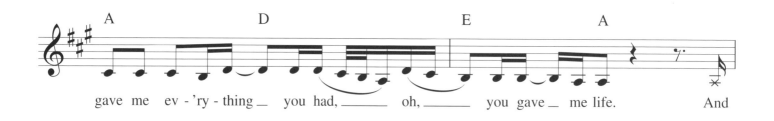

gave me ev - 'ry - thing _ you had, ____ oh, ___ you gave _ me life. And

Chorus

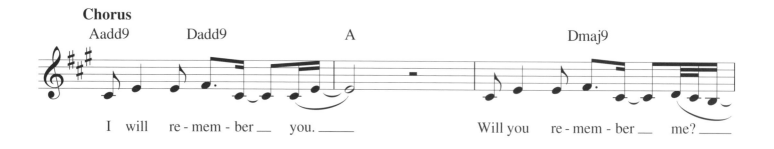

I will re - mem - ber _ you. ___ Will you re - mem - ber _ me? ___

_____ Don't let your life _____ pass _ you by. _

Weep not for _____ the mem - o - ries. _

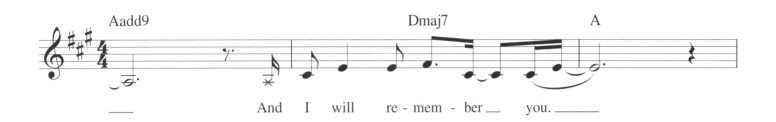

__ And I will re - mem - ber __ you. _____

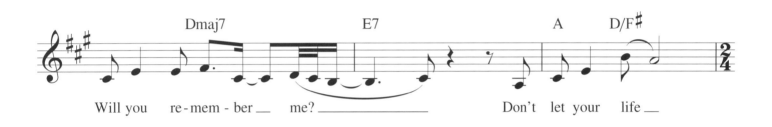

Will you re - mem - ber __ me? _____ Don't let your life __

pass _ you by. _____ Weep not _ for _ the

Outro

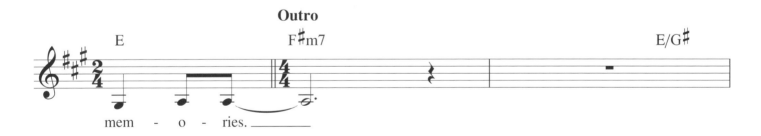

mem - o - ries. _____

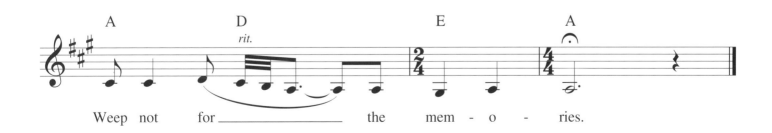

Weep not for _____ the mem - o - ries.

(I've Had)
The Time of My Life

from DIRTY DANCING

Words and Music by Franke Previte, John DeNicola and Donald Markowitz

Intro-Chorus
Moderately

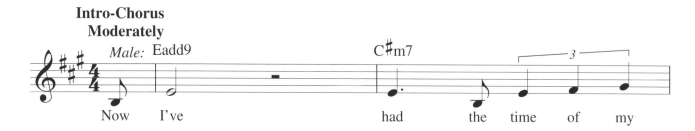

Now I've ... had the time of my

life. ___ No, I nev - er felt ___ like this be - fore. Yes, I

'Cause ___

swear. It's the truth, ___ and I owe it all to you. ___

I've had the time of my life, ___ and I

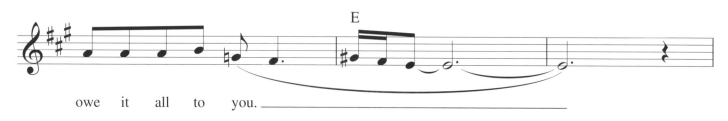

owe it all to you. ___

Verse

Male:

D/E

1. I've been wait-in' for __ so long, _____ now I've

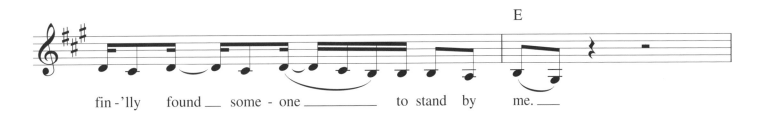

E

fin-'lly found __ some-one _____ to stand by me. __

Female:

D/E

We saw the writ-ing on the wall, _____ and we

E

felt this mag-i-cal __ fan-ta - sy. _____

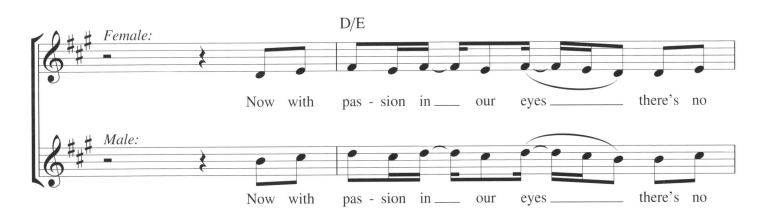

Female:

D/E

Now with pas-sion in __ our eyes _____ there's no

Male:

Now with pas-sion in __ our eyes _____ there's no

E

way we could __ dis-guise __ it se-cret-ly. __ So we

way we could __ dis-guise __ it se-cret-ly. __ So we

take each oth - er's hand __ 'cause we seem to un - der - stand __ the ur - gen -

take each oth - er's hand __ 'cause we seem to un - der - stand __ the ur - gen -

- cy. ___

- cy. ___ Just __ re - mem - ber.

Pre-Chorus

You're the one thing ___

I can't get e - nough

So I'll tell you some - thing. ___

of.

life, _____ and I've searched through ev - 'ry o - pen door 'til I

life, _____ and I've searched through ev - 'ry o - pen door 'til I

found the ___ truth, _____ and I owe it all to you. _____

found the ___ truth, _____ and I owe it all to you. _

Female:

___ 2. With my

Verse

bod - y and soul, _ I'll want you more than you'll ev - er know. _____

Male:

So we'll just let it go, _ don't be a - fraid _ to lose con - trol. _

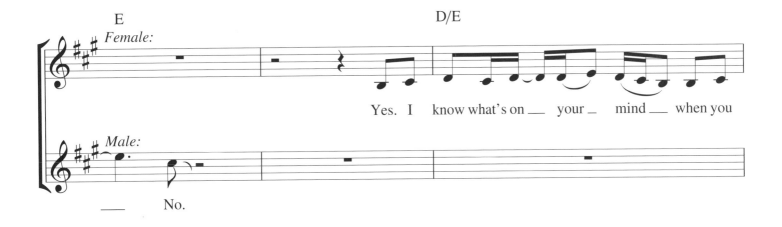

Pre-Chorus

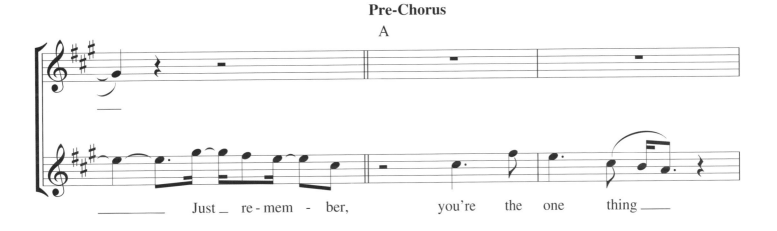

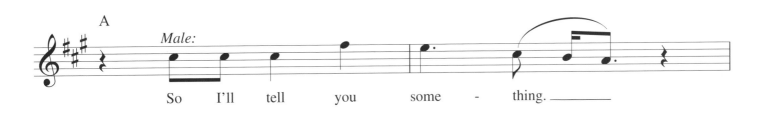

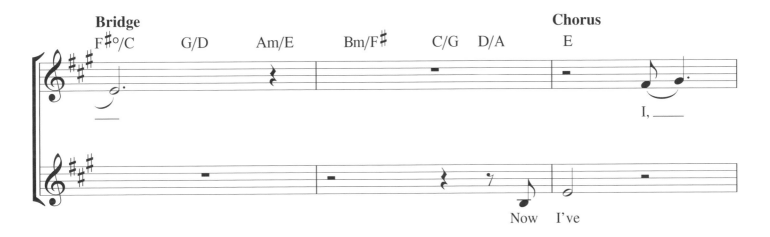

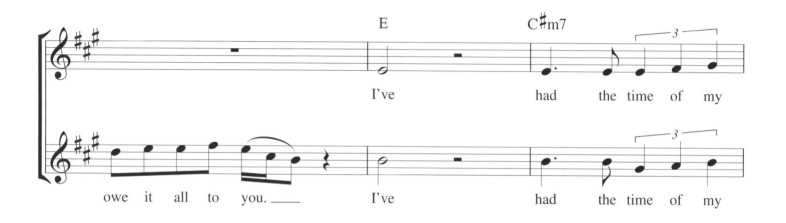

Outro-Chorus

31

The Way We Were

from the Motion Picture THE WAY WE WERE

Words by Alan and Marilyn Bergman
Music by Marvin Hamlisch

___ we __ left be - hind, _____ smiles we gave to one an - oth ___ - ___ er _____

___ of the way ___ we were. _____

Bridge

Can it be _____ that it was all _____ so sim - ple then,

or has time ___ re - writ - ten ev - 'ry _____ line? ___

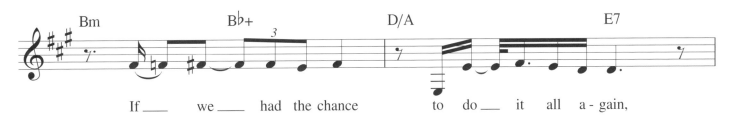

If ___ we ___ had the chance to do ___ it all a - gain,

Verse

tell me, would we? Could we? _____ 3. Mem - 'ries _____

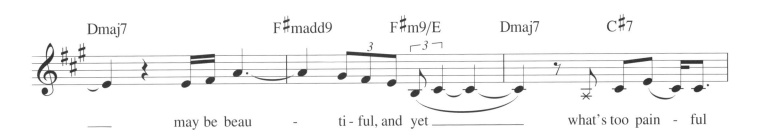

___ may be beau - ti - ful, and yet _____ what's too pain - ful

to re-mem-ber _____ we sim-ply choose _____ to for - get. __

_____ So _____ it's __ the laugh - ter _____ we __ will __

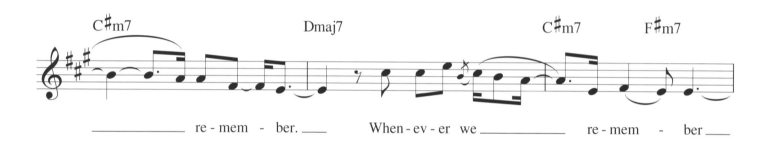

_____ re - mem - ber. __ When - ev - er we _____ re - mem - ber __

Outro

__ the way   we   were. _____ The way __ we

were. _____   Ooh. _____

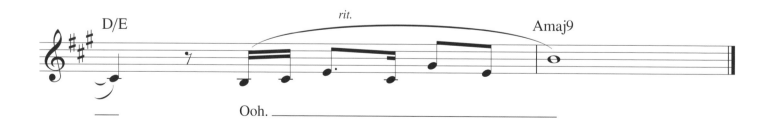

__ Ooh. _____

You Must Love Me

from the Cinergi Motion Picture EVITA

Words by Tim Rice
Music by Andrew Lloyd Webber

Intro
Moderately

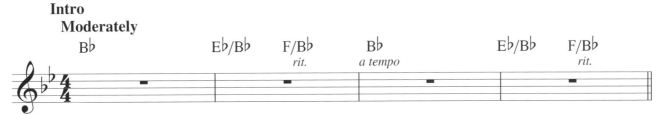

Verse
Slight Rubato

1. Where do we go from here? This is-n't where _ we in-

Moderately

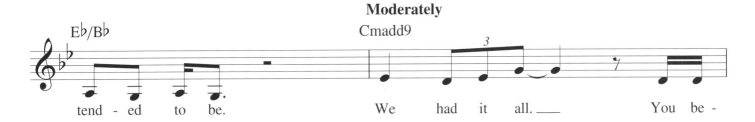

tend - ed to be. We had it all. ___ You be-

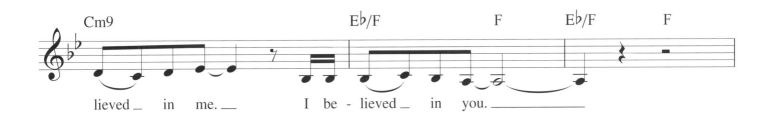

lieved _ in me. ___ I be - lieved _ in you. _____

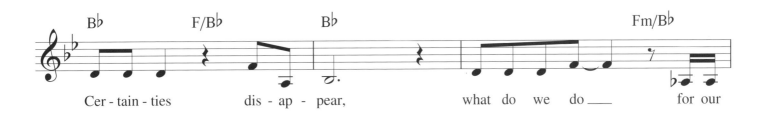

Cer - tain - ties dis - ap - pear, what do we do ___ for our

dream to sur - vive? ___ How do we keep ___ all our pas - sions a - live

as we __ used __ to do? _____ Deep in __ my heart, I'm con-

ceal - ing things that I'm long - ing __ to __ say, __

scared to con-fess what I'm feel - ing, __ fright - ened you'll slip a -

way. You must love me. You must love

Interlude

me.

Verse

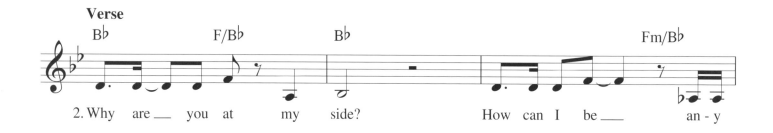

2. Why are __ you at my side? How can I be __ an - y

use to you now? _ Give me a chance _ and I'll let you see how

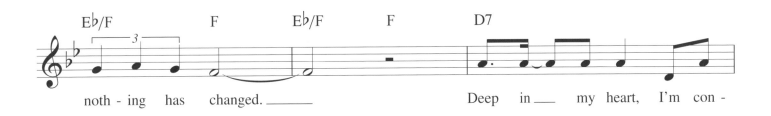

noth - ing has changed. _____ Deep in ___ my heart, I'm con -

ceal - ing things that I'm long - ing to say, ___

scared to con - fess what I'm feel - ing, ___ fright - ened ___ you'll slip a -

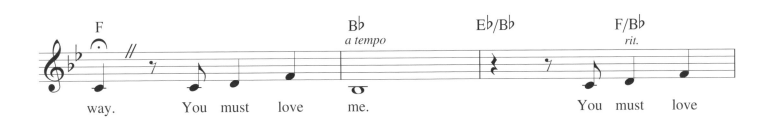

way. You must love me. You must love

me. You must love me.

When I Fall in Love

featured in the TriStar Motion Picture SLEEPLESS IN SEATTLE

from ONE MINUTE TO ZERO

Words by Edward Heyman
Music by Victor Young

Intro
Moderately

Verse
Rubato

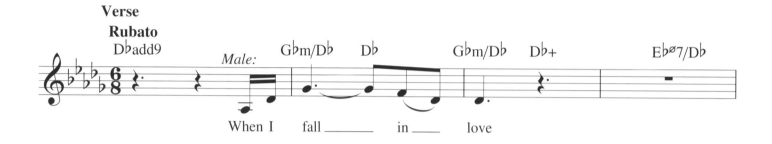

When I fall _____ in _____ love

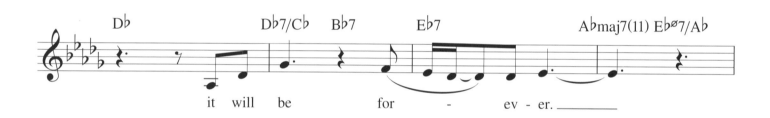

it will be for - ev - er. _____

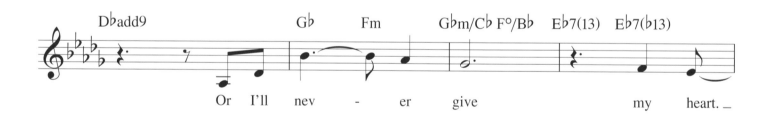

Or I'll nev - er give my heart. _____

_____ In a rest - less world _____ like

this is, _____ love has end - ed _____ be - fore it's _____ be -

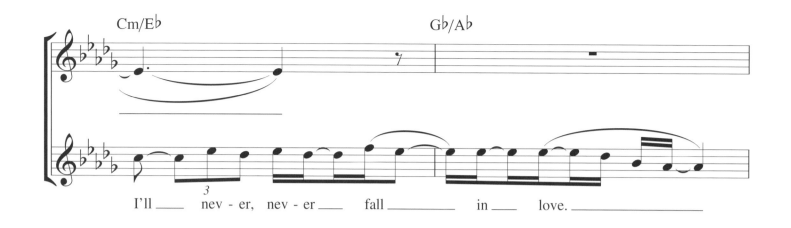

I'll __ nev - er, nev - er __ fall __ in __ love. _____

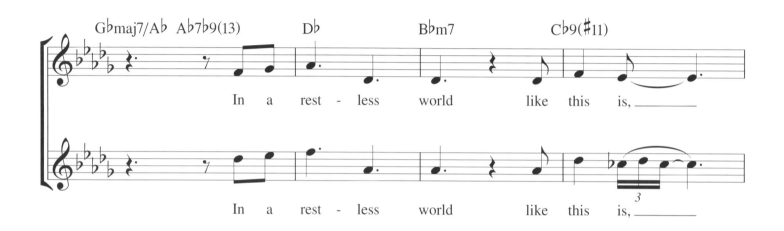

In a rest - less world like this is, _____

In a rest - less world like this is, _____

love has end - ed __ be - fore it's __ be -

love has end - ed __ be - fore it's __ be -

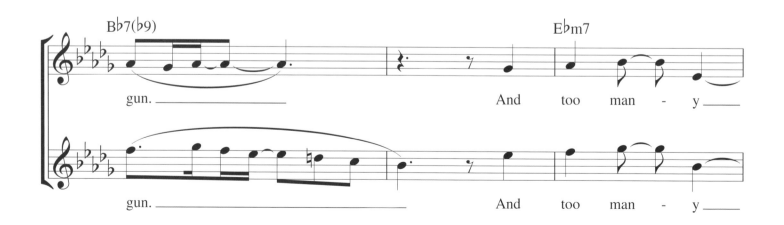

gun. _____ And too man - y _____

gun. _____ And too man - y _____

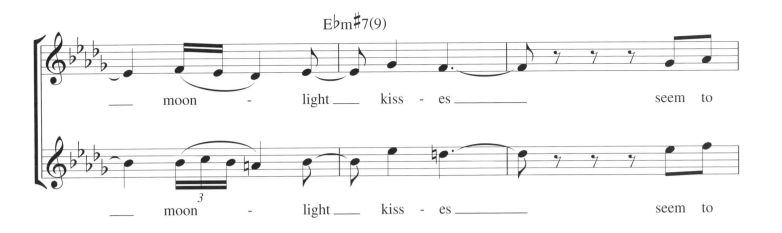

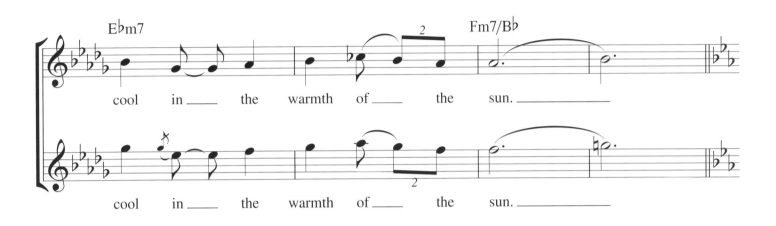

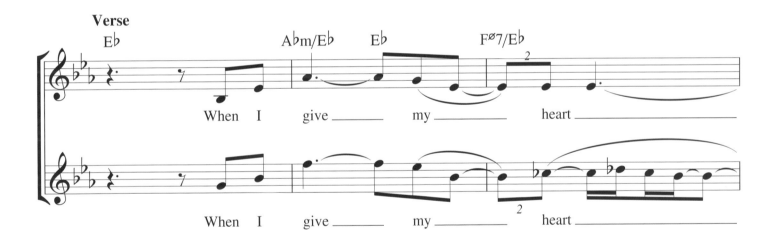

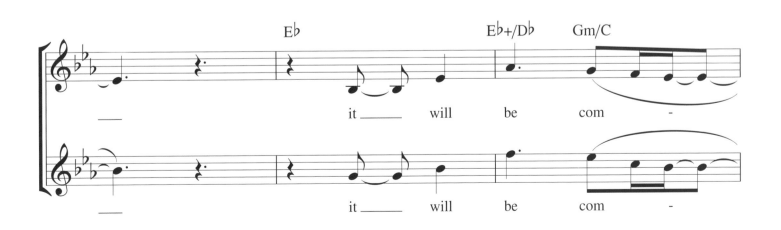

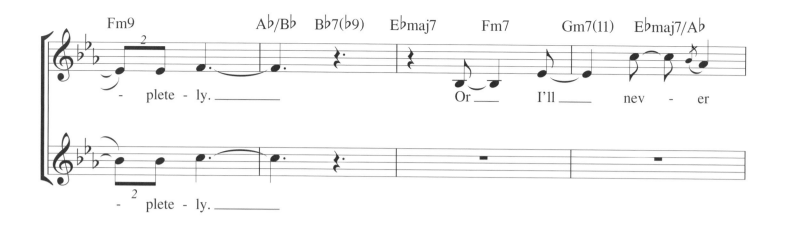

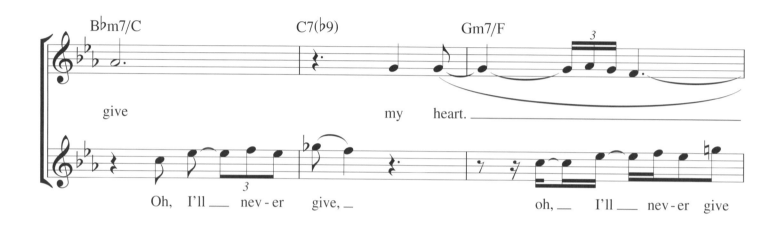

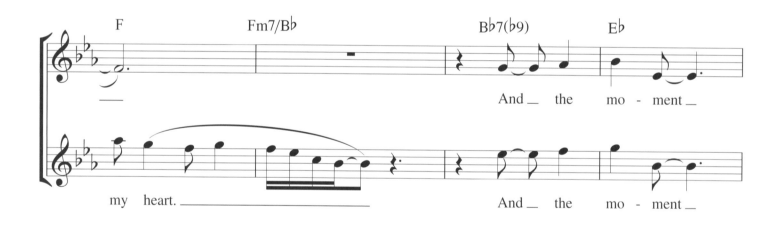

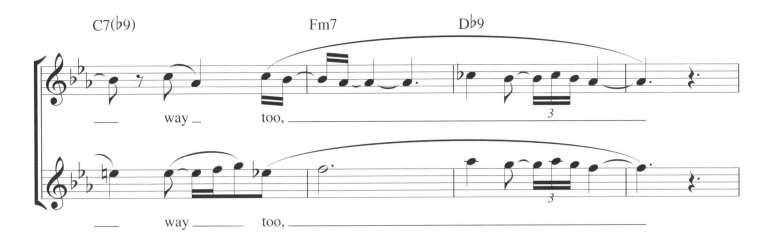

way ___ too, ___

way ___ too, ___

Rubato

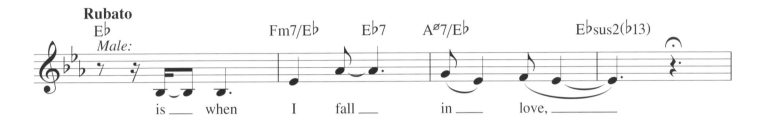

Male:

is ___ when I fall ___ in ___ love, ___

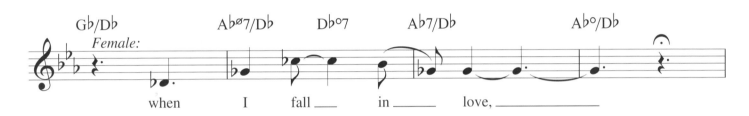

Female:

when I fall ___ in ___ love, ___

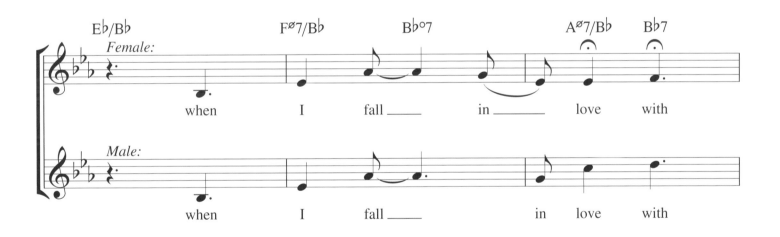

Female:

when I fall ___ in ___ love with

Male:

when I fall ___ in love with

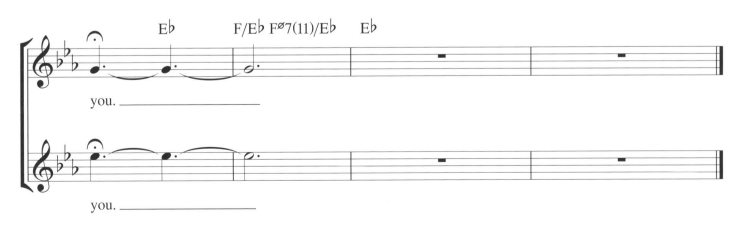

you. ___

you. ___

Pro Vocal® Series
SONGBOOK & SOUND-ALIKE CD
SING 8 CHART-TOPPING SONGS WITH A PROFESSIONAL BAND

Whether you're a karaoke singer or an auditioning professional, the Pro Vocal® series is for you! Each book contains the lyrics, melody, and chord symbols for eight hit songs. The CD contains demos for listening, and separate backing tracks so you can sing along. The CD is playable on any CD player, but it is also enhanced so PC and Mac computer users can adjust the recording to any pitch without changing the tempo! Perfect for home rehearsal, parties, auditions, corporate events, and gigs without a backup band.

ELVIS PRESLEY – VOLUME 1
Blue Suede Shoes • Can't Help Falling in Love • Don't Be Cruel (To a Heart That's True) • Good Luck Charm • I Want You, I Need You, I Love You • Love Me • (Let Me Be Your) Teddy Bear • Treat Me Nice.
00740333 ....$14.95

BROADWAY SONGS
WOMEN'S EDITION
A Change in Me (Beauty and the Beast) • I Can Hear the Bells (Hairspray) • Memory (Cats) • On My Own (Les Misérables) • Someone like You (Jekyll & Hyde) • There Are Worse Things I Could Do (Grease) • Without You (Rent).
00740247 ....$14.95

MEN'S EDITION
Alone at the Drive-In Movie (Grease) • Any Dream Will Do (Joseph and the Amazing Technicolor® Dreamcoat) • Bring Him Home (Les Misérables) • Elaborate Lives (Aida) • Seasons of Love (Rent) • They Live in You (Disney Presents The Lion King: The Broadway Musical) • This Is the Moment (Jekyll & Hyde) • Why God Why? (Miss Saigon).
00740248 ....$14.95

CHRISTMAS STANDARDS
Each song is in the style of the artist listed.

WOMEN'S EDITION
Frosty the Snow Man (Patti Page) • Let It Snow! Let It Snow! Let It Snow! (Lena Horne) • Merry Christmas, Darling (Carpenters) • My Favorite Things (Barbra Streisand) • Rockin' Around the Christmas Tree (Brenda Lee) • Rudolph the Red-Nosed Reindeer (Ella Fitzgerald) • Santa Baby (Eartha Kitt) • Santa Claus Is Comin' to Town (The Andrews Sisters).
00740299 ....$12.95

MEN'S EDITION
Blue Christmas (Elvis Presley) • The Christmas Song (Chestnuts Roasting on an Open Fire) (Nat King Cole) • The Christmas Waltz (Frank Sinatra) • Here Comes Santa Claus (Right down Santa Claus Lane) (Gene Autry) • There's No Place Like) Home for the Holidays (Perry Como) • I'll Be Home for Christmas (Bing Crosby) • Let It Snow! Let It Snow! Let It Snow! (Vaughn Monroe) • Silver Bells (Ray Conniff).
00740298 ....$14.95

CONTEMPORARY HITS
WOMEN'S EDITION
Beautiful (Christina Aguilera) • Breathe (Faith Hill) • Complicated (Avril Lavigne) • Don't Know Why (Norah Jones) • Fallin' (Alicia Keys) • The Game of Love (Santana feat. Michelle Branch) • I Hope You Dance (Lee Ann Womack with Sons of the Desert) • My Heart Will Go On (Celine Dion).
00740246 ....$14.95

MEN'S EDITION
Drive (Incubus) • Drops of Jupiter (Tell Me) (Train) • Fly Away (Lenny Kravitz) • Hanging by a Moment (Lifehouse) • Iris (Goo Goo Dolls) • Smooth (Santana feat. Rob Thomas) • 3 AM (Matchbox 20) • Wherever You Will Go (The Calling).
00740251 ....$14.95

DISCO FEVER
WOMEN'S EDITION
Boogie Oogie Oogie (A Taste of Honey) • Funkytown (Lipps Inc.) • Hot Stuff (Donna Summer) • I Will Survive (Gloria Gaynor) • It's Raining Men (The Weather Girls) • Le Freak (Chic) • Turn the Beat Around (Vicki Sue Robinson) • We Are Family (Sister Sledge).
00740281 ....$12.95

MEN'S EDITION
Boogie Fever (The Sylvers) • Da Ya Think I'm Sexy (Rod Stewart) • Get Down Tonight (KC and the Sunshine Band) • Love Rollercoaster (Ohio Players) • Stayin' Alive (The Bee Gees) • Super Freak (Rick James) • That's the Way (I Like It) (KC and the Sunshine Band) • Y.M.C.A. (Village People).
00740282 ....$12.95

'80s GOLD
WOMEN'S EDITION
Call Me (Blondie) • Flashdance ... What a Feeling (Irene Cara) • Girls Just Want to Have Fun (Cyndi Lauper) • How Will I Know (Whitney Houston) • Material Girl (Madonna) • Mickey (Toni Basil) • Straight Up (Paula Abdul) • Walking on Sunshine (Katrina and the Waves).
00740277 ....$12.95

MEN'S EDITION
Every Breath You Take (The Police) • Heart and Soul (Huey Lewis) • Hurts So Good (John "Cougar") • It's Still Rock and Roll to Me (Billy Joel) • Jessie's Girl (Rick Springfield) • Maneater (Hall & Oates) • Summer of '69 (Bryan Adams) • You Give Love a Bad Name (Bon Jovi).
00740278 ....$12.95

JAZZ STANDARDS
Great jazz classics, each in the style of the artist listed.

WOMEN'S EDITION
Bye Bye Blackbird (Carmen McRae) • Come Rain or Come Shine (Judy Garland) • Fever (Peggy Lee) • The Girl from Ipanema (Astrud Gilberto) • Lullaby of Birdland (Ella Fitzgerald) • My Funny Valentine (Sarah Vaughan) • Stormy Weather (Keeps Rainin' All the Time) (Lena Horne) • Tenderly (Rosemary Clooney).
00740249 ....$14.95

MEN'S EDITION
Ain't Misbehavin' (Louis Armstrong) • Don't Get Around Much Anymore (Tony Bennett) • Fly Me to the Moon (In Other Words) (Frank Sinatra) • Georgia on My Mind (Ray Charles) • I've Got You Under My Skin (Mel Torme) • Misty (Johnny Mathis) • My One and Only Love (Johnny Hartman) • Route 66 (Nat King Cole).
00740250 ....$14.95

Prices, contents, & availability subject to change without notice.

R&B SUPER HITS
WOMEN'S EDITION
Baby Love (The Supremes) • Dancing in the Street (Martha & The Vandellas) • I'm So Excited (Pointer Sisters) • Lady Marmalade (Patty LaBelle) • Midnight Train to Georgia (Gladys Knight & The Pips) • Rescue Me (Fontella Bass) • Respect (Aretha Franklin) • What's Love Got to Do with It (Tina Turner).
00740279 ....$12.95

MEN'S EDITION
Brick House (Commodores) • I Can't Help Myself (Sugar Pie, Honey Bunch) (The Four Tops) • I Got You (I Feel Good) (James Brown) • In the Midnight Hour (Wilson Pickett) • Let's Get It On (Marvin Gaye) • My Girl (The Temptations) • Shining Star (Earth, Wind & Fire) • Superstition (Stevie Wonder).
00740280 ....$12.95

WEDDING GEMS
WOMEN'S EDITION
Grow Old with Me (Mary Chapin Carpenter) • How Beautiful (Twila Paris) • The Power of Love (Celine Dion) • Save the Best for Last (Vanessa Williams) • We've Only Just Begun (Carpenters) • When You Say Nothing at All (Alison Krauss & Union Station) • You Light up My Life (Debby Boone) • You Needed Me (Anne Murray).
00740309 Book/CD Pack $12.95

MEN'S EDITION
Back at One (Brian McKnight) • Butterfly Kisses (Bob Carlisle) • Here and Now (Luther Vandross) • I Will Be Here (Steven Curtis Chapman) • In My Life (The Beatles) • The Keeper of the Stars (Tracy Byrd) • Longer (Dan Fogelberg) • You Raise Me Up (Josh Groban).
00740310 Book/CD Pack $12.95

DUETS EDITION
Don't Know Much (Aaron Neville & Linda Ronstadt) • Endless Love (Diana Ross & Lionel Richie) • From This Moment On (Shania Twain & Bryan White) • I Finally Found Someone (Barbra Streisand & Bryan Adams) • I Pledge My Love (Peaches & Herb) • Nobody Loves Me like You Do (Anne Murray & Dave Loggins) • Tonight, I Celebrate My Love (Peabo Bryson & Roberta Flack) • Up Where We Belong (Joe Cocker & Jennifer Warnes).
00740311 ....$12.95

ANDREW LLOYD WEBBER
WOMEN'S EDITION
All I Ask of You • As If We Never Said Goodbye • Don't Cry for Me Argentina • I Don't Know How to Love Him • Memory • Unexpected Song • Wishing You Were Somehow Here Again • With One Look.
00740348 ....$14.95

MEN'S EDITION
All I Ask of You • Any Dream Will Do • I Only Want to Say (Gethsemane) • Love Changes Everything • Memory • The Music of the Night • No Matter What • On This Night of a Thousand Stars.
00740349 ....$14.95

Visit Hal Leonard online at www.halleonard.com

THE SINGER'S MUSICAL THEATRE ANTHOLOGY

THE WORLD'S MOST TRUSTED SOURCE FOR GREAT THEATRE LITERATURE FOR SINGING ACTORS
Compiled and Edited by Richard Walters

The songs in this series are vocal essentials from classic and contemporary shows – ideal for the auditioning, practicing or performing vocalist. Each of the eighteen books contains songs chosen because of their appropriateness to that particular voice type. All selections are in their authentic form, excerpted from the original vocal scores. Each volume features notes about the shows and songs. There is no duplication between volumes.

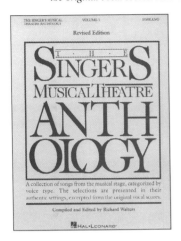

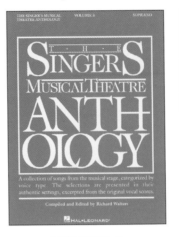

VOLUME 1

SOPRANO
(REVISED EDITION)

47 songs: Where or When • If I Loved You • Goodnight, My Someone • My Funny Valentine • Smoke Gets in Your Eyes • Barbara Song • Till There Was You • Falling in Love with Love • I Could Have Danced All Night • and many more.
00361071 Book Only $19.95
00740227 2 Accompaniment CDs...$22.95

MEZZO-SOPRANO/BELTER
(REVISED EDITION)

39 songs: Anyone Can Whistle • Broadway Baby • Doin' What Comes Naturally • Don't Cry for Me Argentina • Don't Tell Mama • How Are Things in Glocca Morra? • Losing My Mind • Send in the Clowns • and more.
00361072 Book Only $19.95
00740230 2 Accompaniment CDs...$22.95

TENOR
(REVISED EDITION)

40 songs: Being Alive • Johanna • King Herod's Song • Stranger in Paradise • On the Street Where You Live • Younger Than Springtime • Lonely House • Not While I'm Around • Wish You Were Here • and more.
00361073 Book Only $19.95
00740233 2 Accompaniment CDs...$22.95

BARITONE/BASS
(REVISED EDITION)

39 songs: Camelot • C'est Moi • September Song • The Impossible Dream • Lonely Room • Marian the Librarian • Ol' Man River • Soliloquy • Some Enchanted Evening • and more.
00361074 Book Only $19.95
00740236 2 Accompaniment CDs...$22.95

DUETS

21 songs: Too Many Mornings • We Kiss in a Shadow • People Will Say We're in Love • Bess You Is My Woman • Make Believe • more.
00361075 Book Only $17.95
00740239 2 Accompaniment CDs...$22.95

VOLUME 2

SOPRANO
(REVISED EDITION)

42 songs: And This Is My Beloved • How Could I Ever Know • If I Were a Bell • Moonfall • I'll Know • Take Me to the World • The Sound of Music • Unusual Way • Warm All Over • and more.
00747066 Book Only $19.95
00740228 2 Accompaniment CDs...$22.95

MEZZO-SOPRANO/BELTER
(REVISED EDITION)

38 songs: You're the Top • The Party's Over • Adelaide's Lament • I Dreamed a Dream • As Long as He Needs Me • On My Own • I Can Cook Too • If He Walked Into My Life • Never Never Land • Small World • Tell Me on a Sunday • and more.
00747031 Book Only $19.95
00740231 2 Accompaniment CDs...$22.95

TENOR

42 songs: Miracles of Miracles • Sit Down, You're Rockin' the Boat • Bring Him Home • Music of the Night • Close Every Door • All Good Gifts • Anthem • I Belive In You • This Is the Moment • Willkommen • Alone at the Drive-In Movie.
00747032 Book Only $19.95
00740234 2 Accompaniment CDs...$22.95

BARITONE/BASS

40 songs: This Can't Be Love • Bye, Bye Baby • The Surrey with the Fringe on Top • Empty Chairs at Empty Tables • I've Grown Accustomed to Her Face • Stars • My Defenses Are Down • and more.
00747033 Book Only $19.95
00740237 2 Accompaniment CDs...$22.95

DUETS

30 duets, including songs from *Aida, Cabaret, Chicago, Guys and Dolls, Hairspray, The Last Five Years, The Phantom of the Opera, The Producers, Show Boat, Spamalot, Wicked* and more.
00740331 Book Only $19.95
00740240 2 Accompaniment CDs...$22.95

VOLUME 3

SOPRANO

40 songs: Getting to Know You • In My Life • My Favorite Things • Once You Lose Your Heart • Someone to Watch over Me • Think of Me • Whistle Down the Wind • Wishing You Were Somehow Here Again • Wouldn't It Be Loverly • and more.
00740122 Book Only $19.95
00740229 2 Accompaniment CDs...$22.95

MEZZO SOPRANO/BELTER

41 songs: As If We Never Said Goodbye • But Not for Me • Everything's Coming up Roses • I Ain't Down Yet • Maybe This Time • My Heart Belongs to Daddy • Someone like You • Stepsisters' Lament • The Ladies Who Lunch • You Can't Get a Man with a Gun • many more.
00740123 Book Only $19.95
00740232 2 Accompaniment CDs...$22.95

TENOR

35 songs: Almost Like Being in Love • Any Dream Will Do • Corner of the Sky • Hey There • Mama Says • Mister Cellophane • One Song Glory • Steppin' Out with My Baby • Sunset Boulevard • What You'd Call a Dream • Your Eyes • and more.
00740124 Book Only $19.95
00740235 2 Accompaniment CDs...$22.95

BARITONE/BASS

42 songs: All I Care About • Gigi • I Confess • If I Can't Love Her • If I Sing • The Kid Inside • Les Poissons • Lucky to Be Me • Marry Me a Little • Paris by Night • Santa Fe • and more.
00740125 Book Only $19.95
00740238 2 Accompaniment CDs...$22.95

VOLUME 4

SOPRANO

40 songs: Bewitched • Children Will Listen • Home • I Have Dreamed • It's a Most Unusual Day • A Lovely Night • One Boy (Girl) • The Song Is You • Speak Low • We Kiss in a Shadow • Why Do I Love You? • Why Was I Born? • and more.
00000393 Book Only $19.95
00000397 2 Accompaniment CDs...$22.95

MEZZO SOPRANO/BELTER

37 songs: Anything but Lonely • Heaven Help My Heart • I Can Hear the Bells • I Don't Know How to Love Him • Just One Step • Life with Harold • The Man That Got Away • Popular • Roxie • Shadowland • There Are Worse Things I Could Do • The Wizard and I • and more.
00000394 Book Only $19.95
00000398 2 Accompaniment CDs...$22.95

TENOR

37 songs: Awaiting You • Dancing Through Life • Goodnight Saigon • If You Were Gay • Love Changes Everything • A Man Could Go Quite Mad • One Track Mind • Tschaikowsky (And Other Russians) • Who Am I? • You Walk with Me • and more.
00000395 Book Only $19.95
00000399 2 Accompaniment CDs...$22.95

BARITONE/BASS

40 songs: Along Came Bialy • Edelweiss • Get Me to the Church on Time • I'm Not Wearing Underwear Today • A Lot of Livin' to Do • Put on a Happy Face • Wonderful • Ya Got Trouble • and more.
00000396 Book Only $19.95
00000401 2 Accompaniment CDs...$22.95

Prices, contents, and availability are subject to change without notice.

Please visit **www.halleonard.com** for complete contents listings.

FOR MORE INFORMATION, SEE YOUR LOCAL MUSIC DEALER,
OR WRITE TO:

HAL•LEONARD®
CORPORATION

7777 W. BLUEMOUND RD. P.O. BOX 13819 MILWAUKEE, WI 53213

0107